# PICASSO

*Text by*
UMBRO APOLLONIO

*Translated from the Italian by*
CESARE FOLIGNO

CROWN PUBLISHERS, INC. ◄ NEW YORK

# LIST OF ILLUSTRATIONS

I. WOMAN'S HEAD

Spring of 1907. Oil on canvas
André Lefèvre collection, Paris

II. WOMAN SEATED

1909. Oil on canvas, 40" × 33"
Roland Penrose Collection

III. THE WINDOW

Saint-Raphael, 1919
Gouache, 14" × 10"
Private collection

IV. PIERROT AND HARLEQUIN

Juan-les-Pins, 1920
Gouache, $9^5/_8$" × $8^1/_4$"
Paul Rosenberg gallery

V. STILL LIFE WITH JUG
AND FRUIT-DISH

1931. (February 22nd.)
Oil on canvas, 51" × 64"
Henry P. McIlhenny, Germantown

VI. SLEEPING WOMAN
THE DREAM

1932. Oil on canvas, 39" × 52"
W. Ganz Collection, New York

VII. COCK

1938. Pastel, $30^1/_2$" × $21^1/_4$"
The Colin collection, New York

VIII. STILL LIFE WITH A
BLACK BULL'S HEAD

1938. Oil on canvas, $38^1/_2$" × 52"

IX. STILL LIFE OX'S SKULL

1942. Oil on canvas, 39" × 52"
Private collection

X. ALGERIAN WOMEN
(After Delacroix)

1955. Oil on canvas, 46" × 59"
Property of the artist

*COVER PLATE*

## THE LOVERS (Detail)

Oil on canvas. Mr. and Mrs. Harriman's collection, New York.

This gay, brightly coloured picture belongs to the 1920s and is significant for two separate reasons; firstly because such a pleasant, sentimental subject could only have been painted by a happy, light-hearted man, and secondly because the amorous couple look as though they had been caught in a theatrical pose, or a classical ballet *adagio*. In fact the results of Picasso's journey to Italy with Cocteau in 1917 included not only the awakening of his interest in dancing and his meeting with Olga Koklova of the Ballets Russes (whom he married), but also a return to realism and to a liking for traditional disciplines, as exemplified in his series of " large human figures ".

# PICASSO

An artist needs attune himself to his age; nor can artistic culture ever be severed from that complex of spiritual forces which go to the making not only of history, but of man himself.

The world of the spirit is constantly undergoing a crisis, whether this crisis develops smoothly and almost unnoticeably, or whether it is more turbulent and noisy. Few men would deny that, since the first decade of this century, a widespread uncertainty has prevailed concerning the development of art. From this a state of dissatisfaction has arisen which, by degrees, has clearly expressed itself in an open instability and a troubled mind. Nor could it have been otherwise while all forms of existence were questioned and endangered by a solution that looked, and possibly is, still remote. Human institutions could not avoid reacting at a time when the theory of relativity was announced and a fourth dimension and the infinity of space discovered. It would appear as if, during the past centuries, everything had been discovered and no chance left for new inventions. Even though we realize that the boundaries within which artists are necessarily working are a historical reality and as such inescapable, and that in such a reality the struggle between conflicting esthetic theories responds to the changes in a civilization desperately attemping to find a solution to its problems, we must never overlook another reality, the reality of art and the facts of art, however they may be ascertained. In the course of history, even in the most perilous periods of decadence, there always exist some positive elements in which human experience fulfils itself by definite forms and attains the level of a universal language. This is the reason why we are bound to consider Picasso as the most significant artist of this period; for in a way he has transformed a variety of experiences, and thanks to his masterly craftsmanship, succeeded in expressing himself and ourselves in a variety of pictorial languages.

A merely passing glance at the whole range of Picasso's works reveals a most mobile succession of contacts with the various artistic expressions of his age; so that we are left wondering in the end whether what he has given us or what he has taken away from us is more important. Along the secret path of his inspiration he flits from epics to myth, from lyricism to surrealism, from the grotesque to pathos. In an epoch that is wholly opposed to schools and to pre-established forms, in which the grouping of signs is of greater value than their meaning, Picasso is dominant because of his energetic rebellion, his passionate protest, and his inexhaustible inventive power. He fought against himself and against his own recollections in order to rid himself of what he had learned from a centuries-long history, to assert his re-acquired freedom of expression. He may have, at a certain moment, responded to the sternness of Ingres, but he spurned Mondrian's later severity; and not a glance did he cast upon Kandinsky's dynamic and abstract impressionism. His were always longer leaps, more immediately dependent on the suggestions of his own temperament. In this new tradition the data of past ages are summed up, for it is only thus that their teaching can affect us and become valid and effective for us too. Picasso has roamed through those past traditions as if through a maze, and has issued forth so powerfully capable of interpreting and even of adapting those traditions to our age, as to inaugurate one of the most inspired of manners for the revival and realization of what seemed finally exhausted and buried. Even though his activity occasionally turns into a creative rage, into a kind of hatred toward everything that his memory supplies, he finds safety in the precision of his signs and in the number of his works. They form by now a cycle of romances crowded with figures, stories, characters, episodes, faces, and events which are all held together by an unfailing intensity and energy of style. Picasso's works may be recognized some day and read as the novel most truthfully representing the life of our age.

What troubles and disturbs one most in this romance is Picasso's changing manner, which is far more disturbing than the changing figures by which it is in turn represented. Whatever form each of his works may assume, they all possess so strict a unity of style that any hidden change, even the most rudimentary one, finds its proper place in the consistent organism of what his imagination suggests to him. It is always possible to say that a single work is more or less successful, but it is never possible to maintain that it is the result of the juxtaposition of different moments. The mood that inspired it permeates every element of its composition with an unfailing intensity. Had not each of his works originated in a deep-set expressive need, in the closest correlation of his emotion with the reality of life or of culture, neither would such a result have been attained, nor would the artistic quality of his work have been proved. Picasso does not set out as a teacher successively experimenting with different types of pictorial solutions, but he displays a projection of his own and of our inner lives, disturbed as they are by the impact of the often violent, aggressive, and painful events of the day, as well as by the longing for all that is past and regretfully recognized as unavoidably fading away. This is so true that these shiftings, so characteristic of Picasso's creation, constitute the essence of his signification, namely a creative process that avers the persistent feeling of despair by which it has been enabled and compelled to realize itself.

Jaime Sabartés—his friend and secretary for many years—keeping aloof from any subtle critical research, has thus accurately described this contact of Picasso's with the reality that surrounds and inspires him: "...extremely pliable to the impressions he receives, he is prompt in responding to suggestions from anything around him, a flower, a scrap of paper trailing on the ground, and so on. While his senses are ever open to perception, his restlessness, his intelligence, what he has felt and remembers, act together in him. Everything ferments, and nothing stops. None of his manners of expression has ever become a permanent disease. We are often told that he paints like So-and-So. In his case this is a matter of no consequence; he may have collected some germs of infection in passing. That is all; and time will take care of his recovery. It is a matter of a change of air. By incessantly painting and drawing, he forgets anything that his good or ill luck has brought to him. He forgets it, as he forgets the 'when' and the 'how'. Each disease inoculates him with an immunizing serum " [1].

And Picasso himself is supposed to have acknowledged in 1926: " A picture is never a conclusion for me, it is not a ripeness; it is much rather a happy chance and an experience " [2], which does not mean that art, in his view, is an empiric investigation advancing by progressive experiments; but, on the contrary, that real inspiration (" a happy chance ") is at one and the same time a manner of apprehension (" experience "). So much so that he is further supposed to have declared that " facts are to be represented as they are apprehended, rather than as they are seen " [3]. Each stage of vision is merely a decomposition of the reality that is seen—the starting point of a process through which the objective essence of things is logically grasped by an individual awareness. As if there was a casual relation of action and counter-action, the two factors, object and subject, add up to a new final oneness. The naturalistic creative process through which the artist was set face to face with nature is annihilated. The artist is within nature: he no longer gazes upon nature, he actually moves onward in order to grasp it. By stimulating an active force in such a direction Picasso's full expression is inexorably reached; and the inertia of things and facts achieves wider correlations and a peremptory resonance. The fundamental point towards the understanding of Picasso's work is precisely to be seen in this function of his pictorial language. Is is a language that loosely breaks into a speech suspended half-way between reality and metaphor, so independently that only superficial onlookers would interpret it as extravagant. Actually it is merely a heroic striving towards truth, a means by which to maintain a particular state of culture and civilization within the control of the individual.

The name of Picasso's father was José Ruiz Blasco, that of his mother Maria Picasso. His life has been singularly intense and productive. Born in Málaga on October 25, 1881, he was already honorably mentioned at sixteen, when he exhibited his picture *Science et Charité* at the Exhibition of Fine Arts in Madrid. At that time he was deeply influenced by Zurbaran and Velasquez, as he was later to be fascinated by El Greco. From that

[1]  JAIME SEBARTÉS: *Picasso, portraits et souvenirs*, Paris, 1946.

[2]  PABLO PICASSO: *Letter on Art*, in "Ogoniok", Moscow, 1926 Alfred H. Barrr eports in his book, PICASSO: *Fifty Years of his Art*, that the artist, on being definitely questioned, denied the authenticity of this letter. It has been several times reprinted, and has been exploited by many who wished to find corroboration in it for some features of Picasso's art. I shall not trouble to inquire into irs authenticity or to discuss it. Whatever the truth, the statements contained in this letter are perfectly consistent with what his paintings seem to postulate; consequently I do not consider it improper to make use of it.

[3]  Pablo Picasso, quoted above.

time onward, he was never to overlook anything that was most alive, most current and lofty in what culture could offer him, and he was to take his part and to share in this culture. There are no myths and no legends in his life; there is only an absolute dedication to experiments—a few among them unhappy in their result, as necessarily happens to an artist who is a man and not a monster, that is to say a creative artist and not a jobber. But however slight and unpretentious, there was never lacking a feature bearing the stamp of a genuine artistic activity, and thus making its result unfailingly significant.

Much space would be required to give particulars about this formative period, and it may suffice to single out its high spots.

It was impossible for Picasso not to respond to the echoes of the pictorial language of the impressionists at a time when that language was most current and influential, as may be shown by the *Portrait of his Sister* (1889), a variation on Renoir, or his *Boulevard de Clichy* (1901), in Max Pellequer's collection, Paris. Nevertheless, almost at the same time, he was paying attention to Daumier (during his second visit to Paris in 1901 he was able to see the great show of Daumier's works organized by the Ecole des Beaux-Arts and by the Press Syndicate) and to Toulouse-Lautrec. Which means that Picasso, rather than observing schools and tendencies, concentrates his attention upon certain individuals who stand out because of their actual human interests and are less constrained by formal rules, even though these individuals may be less anxious to attain a lyricism tending to chromatic enchantment. Thus, after following in the wake of Sheinlen, he interested himself, while in Paris in 1901, in Van Gogh, Denis, Vuillard, Degas, Renoir, and in Phoenician and Egyptian works, while also being attracted by Gauguin, Tahiti, *Noa-Noa*, Charles Maurice and all that is connected with this style. It was in 1901 that Picasso painted his *Harlequin* (Mr. and Mrs. Clifford's collection, Philadelphia), which clearly anticipates some of the novelties he was later to create.

The beginnings of an artist are always an indication of what his character is. In *El Final*, in the Museum of Modern Art in Barcelona, painted in 1901, the connection with Toulouse-Lautrec is clear, and it was shown already in a menu that Picasso drew for the " Quatre Gats " restaurant in Barcelona in 1898. Critics have often pointed out this connection which is, however, considerably modified in the *Portrait of Jaime Sabartés*, now in the Museum of Modern Art at Moscow, and in the pastel *Women at the Café*, both painted in 1901, in which the placing of the figures, while still dependent on Toulouse-Lautrec's feeling for form, attains a greater autonomy, because of a synthetic setting of the figure within ideal dimensions, entailing a diminished attention to descriptive and illustrative details. Meanwhile, however, as shown by *La nana*, 1901, in the Modern Art Museum of Barcelona, Picasso had not been blind to the new contributions of post-impressionism and even to the formal technique of divisionism. The generous flow of his imagination should not be mistaken for heterogeneous and extemporaneous matter. His sources are not diluted through indolence; they reappear, on the contrary, swollen by the tributaries the painter has met in his progress, and such gaps as are left are due to a temporary straying of the current. And precisely because of this secret flowing, the substance of those sources has been refashioned and has again become productive.

What is now currently described as his " blue period " is to be placed between the end of 1901 and the beginning of 1904. Typical of this period are pain-stricken scenes of unhappy and suffering people in a silent blue tone, almost monochromatic (Rouault was using a similar basic color almost at the same time), with stiff and stern profiles, set in an immobility that is scarcely attenuated by the surrounding and enveloping space.

The influence of El Greco was to be exemplified later and is shown in *The Old Guitar Player*, 1903, of the Chicago Art Institute. Shortly thereafter Picasso settled definitively in Paris, and at first gave himself up to a kind of bohemian life. He visited cafés and cabarets, painted at night, and at the same time formed connections with the leading representatives of art and culture: Reverdy, Salmon, Van Dongen, Degas, Juan Gris, Duhamel, Apollinaire, Gertrude Stein, Matisse, the Douanier Rousseau, and others. He always kept at the center of the keenest and most progressive intellectual life and took an active part in it, even though avoiding every striking gesture; merely by attending, he gave importance to a meeting or to a display. During 1905 he was interested in Puvis de Chavannes and Gauguin. It was from this attention to Gauguin (which is clearly shown in such works of 1906 as the pen-drawing *Andorra Peasants* now in the Chicago Art Institute, the *Self-portrait*, now in the Philadelphia Museum of Art, and the celebrated *Two Nudes* of the Silbermann collection in New York) that, helped by some archaistic suggestions, his cubist manner was to start—a cubist language that had been vaguely foreshadowed in his *Landscape of Barcelona*, 1903 (formerly in the Percier Gallery) and was to display its formal principles to a far greater degree in his *Landscape with Figures* of 1908.

His " pink period ", that followed upon the " blue period ", may be approximately placed between the end of 1905 and 1906. There is a greater tenderness in his work of this period, a kind of restfulness which the artist is contemplating, as if he had transformed the excitement of color and form peculiar to the " fauves " (the " fauves " made their first appearance in 1905 at the Salon d'Automne) into a more subtle sentiment through the intervention, as it were, of Greek refinement. It was at this time that Picasso discovered the old Grecian serenity (see *La toilette*, 1906, in the Albright Art Gallery at Buffalo) which he was not readily to forget, since this delicate and correct manner was, in later years, occasionally to interrupt his most raging and monstrous pictures.

During 1906 he reflected upon the great teaching of Cézanne; and later, in 1909, the portrait of Clovis Sagot (in the A. E. von Saher collection of Amsterdam) was to represent an echo of that teaching and show that the cubist order was mainly promoted by it; for, after all, the portrait of Braque was painted in that year. He meditated on the ancient sculptures of Spain he saw in the Louvre, and painted in the same year the *Portrait of Gertrude Stein*, now in the Metropolitan Museum of New York. In the following year he met Braque and Derain and, towards the end of 1907, he became interested in negro sculpture and painted *Les demoiselles d'Avignon* (in the Museum of Modern Art in New York). This work of primary importance from which originated the most pointed novelty in the pictorial language of our time marks the beginning of Picasso's most decisive step towards the cubist concept.

In 1908 are found with him Braque, Metzinger, Salmon, Apollinaire, Raynal, Princet (a professor of mathematics), Gris and Kahnweiler, representatives of the group by which the first truly significant principles of cubism were to be posited, either from an esthetic or from a conceptual and critical viewpoint according to their individual professions. From 1909 to 1912 Picasso's creative activity was directed to what has been termed analytical cubism. Later, and until 1921, his inexhaustible productivity brought about the culminating period of the socalled synthetic cubism that had some connection with the forms established by Seurat. Almost at the same time, however, Picasso took notice of the rigorous Ingres, and, soon after making a visit to Italy because of the ballets of Sergei Diaghilev, and above all during his stay at Dinard, his inspiration turned to a sharper renewal of the classical spirit. But, as Sabartés has said, this episode was not destined to last. For, as early as 1925, he was attracted by the theories of the surrealists, even though their attraction was never great for him and was mainly the result of intellectual curiosity. Henceforward his maturity reached exceptional and extraordinary achievements, far beyond the ideologies of the cubists and surrealists.

Picasso does not brook compulsion of any kind; everything under the sway of his mind is refashioned, for he listens to the advice, most authentic and true, that human suggestions press on him. Thus we see an ironical brutality (*Seated Woman with a Fish-like Hat*, 1942), the expressionistic horror of figures (*Seated Nude*, 1940), and even some leanings towards the pure abstract, from which not a few artists drew their often mechanical, if poetically intended, applications (*Guitar*, a carbon of 1912 in the Rosenwald collection; *Le guéridon blanc*, 1920, in the Pellequer collection; the famous pen-drawing of 1926 later reproduced in wood-cut in *Le chef d'œuvre inconnu* of Balzac, and *Musical Instruments*, 1927). The drive towards the initial cubistic concept never abated in him, and even recently, in the figures of 1953, there appear stylistic problems of space and light, separated by violent contrasts in a personified, elementary composition, that is a true transition from the object in reality to the substance of imagination. Certain still-lifes of 1922 or a work like the *Painting Lesson* of 1925 (Paul Rosenberg collection) may be safely compared with *Reading Woman* or *Reading on a Red Background* of 1953. There is in Picasso a moral law that drives him to reach beyond every earthly and cultural myth to avail himself of what is not yet burned out, and above all of his heartfelt experiences. He has discarded any suggestion of his imagination. Every technique—painting, drawing, engraving, sculpture, ceramic (he produced truly exceptional works even in the two latter mediums, although we cannot consider them here)—and also mixed techniques have provided him with the means to discover a point of contact with the failing world (*Charnel-House*, 1944-48; *Massacre in Korea*, 1951; *War and Peace*, 1952). He found contact also with saving poetry (*Ma Jolie*, 1914; André Lefèvre collection, Paris; *Paul Dressed as Pierrot*, 1925; *The Enamelled Kitchen-pot*, 1945, in the Musée National d'Art Moderne, Paris). He was able, for all these reasons, to declare that when cubism was invented there was no intention of inventing cubism, but only of expressing what was in the artist's mind.

1937 was the year of *Guernica* (now in the Museum of Modern Art in New York). Quite apart from the moral and political impulse which suggested this work, which has by now become one among the most celebrated of the modern age, it is worth recalling that the formal and ideal motifs which constitute it go back to more remote antecedents than is generally believed. Consequently it is not merely a work improvised under the stimulus of moral indignation towards a hated cause, and thus by a political impulse. For, in order thoroughly to understand it, without in any way detracting from its value as a moral protest, it will be helpful to look back to the *Bull-fights* of 1917 and 1921, to the *Wounded Horse* of 1923, to the *Crucifixion* of 1930, to the *Bull* of 1934 (Keith Warner collection), to the *Fight with the Minotaur* of 1953 (Henry P. McIlhenny collection, Germantown). They are works revealing in their form and content a similar feeling, if one takes into account, as one should, the necessary and legitimate changes in the artist's experience. One should never forget that changes in Picasso are more apparent than substantial, provided his earliest period is left out, the period ending about 1907 when *Les demoiselles d'Avignon* was produced. All the so-called irreconcilable diversities in works of the same year or of the same period, with which the artist has been taxed by some critics, appear to be easily bridged over when more closely examined, if the stylistic energy which is the most appreciable and determining feature of Picasso's art is more widely and comprehensively understood. The *Three Musicians*, 1921 (in the Museum of Modern Art of New York) and certain *Motherhoods* of the same time manifest a partition of space, a reduction of the plastic elements, a rhythmic articulation that are not contradictory, but are on the contrary the results of a consistent development. The ligature, partly ornamental and partly pointedly straining towards the strongly expressionistic pattern of some of his works of 1938, merely responds, in the end, to an analogous process with results that are, at one and the same time, merciful and grotesque. This interrelationship, despite all contrary appearances, is paralleled by the order in which the motifs and the colours are articulated. Consequently *Guernica* is the work by which Picasso's capabilities can be truly measured, because of the sincerity to which it owes its existence and because of the study to which it owes its form. It is perfect because of the balanced composition by which it is supported even in the minutest details of its strict unity of style, and because it is broad in its inspiration even though tormented and howling. Thus it is a compendium of all the qualities of form and content of Picasso's art: the development of an expressionistic synthesis from the data of nature, lines of force straining to their utmost and breaking out of the frame of the picture, hard and angular contours expressed by a continous and significant play of white, black, and grey (" One works with few colours ", Picasso has said, " but, when each of them is set in its proper place they appear to be many more ") [1]. It is also a statement of Picasso's universal position— his merging every single individuality into a symbol for the whole of humanity.

Picasso is averse to the imitation of nature in every form. He trust in the expressive power of the image cut adrift from nature by a direct, crude, almost savage intrusion of the sweeping force of emotion, even though this intrusion may be conscious and controlled by the rules of craftsmanship. And thus he tends to establish an indissoluble and almost inescapable relation with his confidence in the certainty of the artistic signification which fantasy supplies. He has arranged, at one and the same time, layers of lyricism and prose into a unity of tone and colour which ultimately is the real significance of an artist and of his work for humanity. Only in such a way and by such means may a work aim, despite the restlessness of its problems, at a poetic triumph and a cultural supremacy—two goals in the unending course of civilization and history which have always been linked. By such solution even the most contradictory assertions may be reconciled. The connecting link exists and persists in a loftier need for freedom which, though unavoidably dependent on circumstances, finds in these circumstances the impetus toward the reunion of life with art. " There are painters who change the sun into a yellow spot; but there are others who, thanks to their craftsmanship and intelligence, turn a yellow spot into the sun " [2]. Picasso belongs to the latter breed; for his every line and colour are loaded with life, and call for eyes that meet and penetrate life, just as the artist has met it, penetrated it, and expressed it, without any kind of inhibition and perhaps without any kind of hope.

---

[1] *Conversation avec Picasso* in "Cahiers d'Art", 1935, vol. X, no. 10, pp. 173-78
[2] Pablo Picasso, quoted above.

I

WOMAN'S HEAD

Spring of 1907. Oil on canvas. André Lefèvre collection, Paris.

Picasso spent the summer of 1906 at Gosol in the Andorra valley and brought to an end the period that is called " pink ", because this hue, which he had used in his pictures since the end of the previous year, acquired a warmer tone and tended to red. The picture which is reproduced here is one of the several studies that preceded the composition of that great work, in which the blue and pink tones which Picasso had tried out in the periods that take their names from them are placed side by side without contrast. The synthesis of the figure which is reduced to well-defined chromatic planes, the colors which are distended and yet vibrating, a shaft of light on the face, some black touches framing the profile and the eyes, build up, by means of abstract elements, the presentation of a feeling that is no longer naturalistic, but already expressionistic or otherwise responsive to the fear and the disturbing force of humanity in all that is the deepest and least apparent in it.

## II

### WOMAN SEATED

1909.  Oil on canvas, 40" × 33".  Roland Penrose collection.

In 1909 Picasso was no longer just " a dabbler in paints from Bateau-Lavoir ", whom critics and collectors could well afford to ignore, since by then Vollard had bought enough of his canvases to enable him to move into an apartment in the Boulevard de Clichy with Fernande Olivier.  There he lived during his first period of analytical cubism, in which style he painted several portraits, this being the first.  Roland Penrose has rightly pointed out that " the contrasting greens and red-browns belong to the Provençal landscape of the painter from Aix ".  Later he abandoned the vibrant greens and blues but, as in his portrait of Vollard, accentuated the dissolution of perspective required by the dictates of analysis.

II

III

THE WINDOW

Saint-Raphael, 1919.  Gouache, 14" × 10".  Private collection.

A cubist image, no less than any other image produced by pictorial imagination, unless it is sustained by an adequately strong lyrical inspiration, may be reduced to the enjoyment of an elegant and ornate organism.  This work reveals precisely such a peculiar condition in the artist, who is undecided between reality and imagination and restrains his most genuine impulse.

After his visit to Italy in 1917, Picasso had initiated a singular revival of the classical spirit, to which he had given a solution that decomposed the exquisite structures of ancient tradition in a monumental sense.  He had gazed upon Pompeian paintings and had, perhaps, been slightly impressed by the sort of illusionism they display.

This window which opens on a seascape represented with an almost naturalistic refinement, and through which sunlight comes, in giving relief to the table and to the object on it, if carefully observed, appears to be connected with fore-shortening conceptions that are rather alien to the principles Picasso had adopted since he had initiated the cubistic formula. It was a moment during which Picasso, feeling the call of the classics and yet mindful of the expressive novelties he had discovered, was searching for an agreement in which moderation might overcome the absolute freedom of creation.  The work, while most delicately articulating structure and colour, looks on the whole a little ambiguous.  The window stands as an example of a whole series of analogous compositions, some of which are more definitely cubistic, and some more decidedly inspired.

IV

PIERROT AND HARLEQUIN

Juan-les-Pins, 1920. Gouache, $9\,^5/_8$" × $8\,^1/_4$". Paul Rosenberg gallery.

It was in 1917 that Picasso began to be interested in masks and harlequins, when he prepared the scenery and the costumes for a ballet, *Parade*, on a subject written by Jean Cocteau, set to music by Eric Satie and arranged by Léonide Massine. He had by then already gone through the experience of so-called analytic cubism and was going through the last stage of so-called synthetic cubism—the former representing a real object in its plastic developments looked upon from different points of view; the latter reducing the representation into a single plane by means of emblematic solutions, the meaning of which was rendered evident by distributing the colours into well-defined zones.

This picture of *Pierrot and Harlequin* avoids the precise definition of reality in any way, and the logic of its expression exlusively depends on the colour rhythm and on the connection of fore-shortened planes.

V

STILL LIFE WITH JUG AND FRUIT-DISH

1931. (February 22nd.) Oil on canvas, 51" × 64".
Henry P. McIlhenny collection, Germantown.


It has already been remarked that, for a period which may be said to begin in 1906, Picasso was constantly torn between the postulates of the Greek tradition and his own experimental results achieved through the overpowering need to find a newer and more current pictorial language, wihch can be traced as far back as 1907.

This still life, whose inspiration and linear and chromatic execution are similiar to those of *The Lamp* of the same year, is conceived like medieval stained-glass, both because of the marked partition of the colours, through which the sun shines from behind the canvas, and because of the enclosing of the coloured segments that clearly recalls the strips of lead by which the stained-glass tesserae are kept in place. The power of the image he presents becomes suggestive because its elements are rhythmically composed and the immediacy of his lyric inspiration is self-evident. As always in Picasso's work the main features are the poetic intensity, the total surrender to the creative action, and the harmonious apprehension by which the mind of the artist is sustained in his moments of authentic ecstasy.

VI

SLEEPING WOMAN – THE DREAM

1932. Oil on canvas, 39" × 52". W. Ganz collection, New York.

    This work should be considered in conjunction with other well-known Picassos of the same year, such as *Young Girl sitting in a Red Armchair* and *Nude on a Black Divan*. At this time Picasso, his fame and wealth comfortably established, had excluded unpleasantness from his life; yet he still found a source of happiness outside his marriage in the company of Marie-Thérèse, who bore him a daughter, Maïa, and whose youthful serenity and harmonious blonde beauty inspired him to paint syntheses of arabesques, oriental delicacy, mural decoration, planes and colours in which his appealing brand of cubism penetrates the graphic style of the " full-face and profile ".

25.12.49.

## VII

### COCK

1938. Pastel 30½" × 21¼". The Colin collection, New York.

It is difficult to say whether this cock, so proud of its own appearance, is more afraid of itself or of the symbol it may embody. Barr reports that Picasso, on being visited in his studio by the American painter Xavier Gonzales while he was painting one of these subjects told Gonzales: " There have always been cocks, but like everything else in life, they need to be discovered; just as Corot discovered the morning and Renoir discovered women... We have always seen cocks, but we have never seen them so well as on the weather-cocks of America ".

The propensity to trace a grotesque expression in every human condition which Picasso has felt since the beginning of his artistic growth is ekplicitly stated in those words. The aggressiveness in the attitude and in the eye, which are consistent in their forms, represent, despite the summary stylistic execution, an image which by displaying its strength reveals its inner ludicrous weakness.

VIII

STILL LIFE WITH A BLACK BULL'S HEAD

1938. Oil on canvas, 38½" × 52".

This work was almost unknown until 1944 when it was exhibited in Paris at the " Salon de la Libération". Because of its strictly rhythmical composition and its refined chromatic taste it deserves to be reckoned among the best that Picasso has created.

There are elements in the background, mainly on the right, in which a cubistic conceptualism is traceable, and others, mainly on the left, that are interpreted in a more surrealistic manner. In contrast with all of them there stands out the striking black head of a bull—symbolizing, as Picasso has stated himself, obtuse brutality and destruction—which is very similar to the bull's head in *Guernica*. A flash of pointedly instantaneous poetic evocation lights up the transitions from one object to the other, from an underlying ethical meaning to its stylistic transposition.

VIII

IX

STILL LIFE – OX'S SKULL

1942.  Oil on canvas, 39" × 52".  Private collection.


When the horrors of the Spanish Civil War were revived on an even greater scale with the start of the Second World War, no civilian was more profoundly shaken than Picasso, as a Spaniard, and as an artist.  This was no time for " voluptuous death ", but an apocalypse of bloody annihilation, which banished all hope of happiness or peaceful existence. Impelled to express in painting his horror at this cataclysm and tragedy, Picasso chose skeletons, skulls, etc. as symbols of his hatred and his anguish.  His most tortured figures also date from this period.

X

ALGERIAN WOMEN (after Delacroix)

1955.  Oil on canvas, 46" × 59".  Property of the artist.

    This is one of the most outstanding of his many "variation" pictures - works executed with a famous painting in mind.  (Delacroix's *Algerian Women* was followed in 1957 by Velasquez's *Menines*).  Picasso seems to dissect, paraphrase and adopt, as though he some-how needed to attain inner repose through the creation of  these  dazzling, paradoxical stylistic exercises – his own effective contributions to the undisputed masterpieces which he openly and passionately admired.

X. ALGERIAN WOMEN